Teen Guide to
VOLUNTEERING

Stuart A. Kallen

ReferencePoint
Press®

San Diego, CA

© 2021 ReferencePoint Press, Inc.
Printed in the United States

For more information, contact:
ReferencePoint Press, Inc.
PO Box 27779
San Diego, CA 92198
www.ReferencePointPress.com

LIBRARY OF CONGRESS CATALOGING-IN-PUBLICATION DATA

Names: Kallen, Stuart A., 1955- author.
Title: Teen guide to volunteering / by Stuart A. Kallen.
Description: San Diego : ReferencePoint Press, 2020. | Includes
    bibliographical references and index.
Identifiers: LCCN 2020017071 (print) | LCCN 2020017072 (ebook) | ISBN
    9781682829370 (library binding) | ISBN 9781682829387 (ebook)
Subjects: LCSH: Teenage volunteers in social service--Juvenile literature.
    | Voluntarism--Juvenile literature. | Social action--Juvenile
    literature. | Self-realization--Juvenile literature.
Classification: LCC HV40.42 .K35 2020 (print) | LCC HV40.42 (ebook) | DDC
    361.3/70973--dc23
LC record available at https://lccn.loc.gov/2020017071
LC ebook record available at https://lccn.loc.gov/2020017072

CONTENTS

Help Needed Everywhere

In 2019 the average American teenager spent more than seven hours a day online. That's nearly one-third of every day! Even teens believe they are too attached to their phones. According to a survey by Pew Research, 60 percent of teenagers between the ages of thirteen and seventeen said spending too much time online was a major problem for their generation.

> "Volunteering could be life-changing and even life-saving for those that do it regularly."[2]
>
> —Megan Bailey, volunteer coordinator

If you are concerned about spending half your waking life staring at a cell phone, one option is to volunteer. "There are a gazillion benefits of being a volunteer,"[1] says Debra Weinman, a United Way volunteer engagement manager. One of those benefits is that volunteers make peoples' lives better. And a second benefit is self-directed: people who help others often help themselves. Volunteers usually feel personal satisfaction when they see how their efforts are making the world a better place. Volunteering is also a powerful tool for reducing stress, combating depression, and providing a sense of purpose. As volunteer coordinator Megan Bailey writes, "When teens or young adults volunteer, they develop self-esteem, confidence, and feelings of self-worth. . . . Volunteering could be life-changing and even life-saving for those that do it regularly."[2]

Volunteer work can be challenging. It means giving up your free time to work hard for no pay to help other people or a cause. But most volunteers feel the benefits outweigh the challenges.

When they tackle problems or aid strangers, they often meet like-minded people of all ages from a wide variety of backgrounds. These interactions often reduce feelings of loneliness. Volunteering can also help you widen your social circle beyond your immediate family while forming bonds that last a lifetime. And it is a great way to meet mentors and attain letters of recommendation for college applications.

Lower Your Stress and Develop Skills

Numerous studies show that people who get out of the house and establish strong social connections with others have better over-all health. Kaleigh Rogers volunteers at a therapeutic horse-riding program for children with disabilities in New York City. Rogers

A little girl with special needs learns her way around a horse. Teenagers who volunteer their time working with these children, or doing any other volunteer work, develop skills, insight, and empathy.

describes how she benefits from volunteering: "Whenever I help out at the horse barn, my stress and anxiety levels noticeably drop. I feel calmer, more relaxed, and my mind is clear, often for the first time in weeks. It has quickly become one of the most reliable ways for me to de-stress—I've found it more effective than meditation, medication, or exercise."[3]

Volunteering can help young people find a passion in life while opening a window onto the world of work. Volunteers develop soft skills, or people skills, including tact, patience, the ability to communicate clearly, teamwork, and leadership. Volunteering also teaches hard skills such as how to raise money, manage an organization, promote events, analyze budgets, and raise awareness on social media. And volunteers show a willingness to step outside their comfort zone to advance a larger goal, which is considered a valuable resource by future employers.

Gain Confidence, Empathy, and Courage

There is a widespread notion that most teenagers are self-absorbed. But research has shown this stereotype to be a myth. Studies of adolescent brains using neuroimaging techniques like magnetic resonance imaging (MRI) show that areas of the brain activated by social interactions develop quickly during the teenage years. Researcher Meghan Lynch Forder explains: "This development increases young people's ability to understand the feelings and perspectives of other people . . . to determine whom and how to help."[4] Understanding and helping others is the opposite of being self-centered.

Studies show that helping others increases production of a hormone called oxytocin in the brain. This chemical is sometimes referred to as the love hormone, because it spikes when people bond with friends or snuggle with mates. But it does not take a brain scientist to understand why people feel good from volunteering. The desire to help others is a natural human instinct, and the need is greater than ever before. While some people spend their days complaining on social media about the many difficulties confronting society, others are donating their time and efforts to alleviating those problems. And volunteers are needed almost everywhere. Whether your focus is people, animals, education, the arts, the environment, or some other worthwhile cause that needs attention, volunteering makes the world a better place. As the Tibetan spiritual leader the Dalai Lama says, "When you care for others, you manifest an inner strength despite any difficulties you face. Your own problems will seem less significant and bothersome to you. Reaching beyond your own problems and taking care of others, you gain confidence, courage, and a greater sense of calm."[5]

"Reaching beyond your own problems and taking care of others, you gain confidence, courage, and a greater sense of calm."[5]

—The Dalai Lama, Tibetan spiritual leader

CHAPTER ONE

Volunteer Close to Home

When you envision volunteers, you might picture people handing out bottled water after a natural disaster or dishing up turkey and mashed potatoes at homeless shelters on Thanksgiving. And plenty of volunteers perform such tasks. But some volunteers make the world a better place without leaving their neighborhood, or even their house. If you are just taking your first steps into the world of volunteering, you can look close to home for ways to help others. You might find that you can volunteer without maxing out your schedule or making a long-term commitment.

In 2017, high school student Michelle Lemieux cleaned out her closet for charity. She donated a used prom gown and other accessories to a group called Catherine's Closet that provides formal wear to students who cannot afford to buy the items. Catherine's Closet, founded in 2002, was named after Catherine Johnson, an honor student and valedictorian of her high school class in East Orange, New Jersey. Johnson was killed in a car crash and was buried in the gown she never got to wear to prom.

Lemieux saw Catherine's Closet as a perfect opportunity to volunteer—and she got others to join her:

> I used social media to spread the word locally and collected 58 dresses, plus accessories. My house was filled to the brim with gowns—it was amazing! . . . I witnessed a mother cry as she watched her daughter find the perfect gown for her prom. . . . I was so thrilled to see so many girls and women walk out of the event not just with gowns, but many of the ones I knew came from my friends and community.[6]

Many of the gowns Lemieux collected were from big-name designers like Vera Wang, Ralph Lauren, and Michael Kors. After collecting the formal wear, Lemieux worked with other student volunteers to sort through the dresses and assist customers on distribution days that were held before prom season began.

Catherine's Closet, which also collects toys and books, is active in New Jersey, New York, and Arizona. By 2020, over sixteen thousand girls had benefited from the group's efforts. There are dozens of other organizations that depend on volunteers like Lemieux, people who are willing to spend a few hours sorting through unwanted items, boxing them up, and donating them to people in need.

Other groups provide services similar to Catherine's Closet. Becca's Closet, which operates volunteer-led chapters throughout

> "I was so thrilled to see so many girls and women walk out of the event not just with gowns, but many of the ones I knew came from my friends and community."[6]
>
> —Michelle Lemieux, student volunteer

A Utah teenager who helped start a chapter of Becca's Closet shows off some of the prom dresses that will be given to students who would not otherwise be able to afford a dress for the high school prom.

the country, gives away prom dresses, shoes, accessories, tuxedos, suits, ties, and more to young women and men. In California, Maria's Closet hosts dress drives, while Project GLAM is active on the East Coast. Beyond formal wear, groups such as the Vietnam Vets of America, St. Vincent de Paul, and The Arc are always in need of donated items, including toys, furniture, tablecloths, towels, bedding, and unopened toiletries. Sometimes donation boxes for nonprofit groups can be found outside supermarkets and government buildings, making it easy to donate items to local organizations.

Neighbor to Neighbor

Donating to Catherine's Closet is one of several volunteer projects undertaken by Lemieux. She also puts in time at the local chapter of Neighbors Helping Neighbors (NHN). This organization, which is active in many communities, connects volunteers to older and disabled homeowners, or anyone who has trouble affording home repairs. Volunteers for NHN trim trees, rake leaves, clean gutters, and even fix roofs and paint houses. In cold climates, volunteers remove snow from driveways and sidewalks.

You can offer to shovel a driveway or do housework for a neighbor in need without joining NHN. A quick walk around your neighborhood might reveal a yard that needs maintenance or a house that looks in need of repair. You can also post a notice on a neighborhood's social networking site such as Nextdoor or Front Porch Forum. A help-offered post should include your age, your general location, and the tasks you are willing to perform as a volunteer for neighbors in need.

In 2018, Jacob Shoulders of Orting, Washington, found a great way to help an older neighbor named Paul. Shoulders said his mother always told him to stop and chat with an elderly person he sees sitting alone. After striking up a conversation with Paul, Shoulders learned that the man's roof leaked, which is a big problem for anyone who lives in rainy Washington. Shoulders

Clean Out That Closet

While cleaning out closets is never high on anyone's list of fun things to do, it is a great way to find clothes, toys, and other items at home that can be donated to those in need. The best way to approach closet cleaning is to commit to a date, mark it on your calendar, set an alarm, and make it a priority to follow through. Marie Kondo, who is widely known as a professional organizer, has some closet cleaning tips based on methods she calls the KonMari way. Kondo believes that being neat and well organized brings joy. Writer Murphy Moroney explains how to clean out closets using the KonMari way: "Hold up each item and ask yourself whether or not it sparks joy for you. Start with things that feel easy—the ones that make you feel an immediate 'yes!' or 'no!'—before tackling the trickier items." If an item does not spark joy, or if you have not worn it for a year or more, toss it on the donate pile. Whatever method suits you best, it should not take more than a few hours to separate your clothes into three categories: keep, donate, toss. Sharing with others what you no longer use is a simple way to help people in your community.

Murphy Moroney, "Declutter Your Family's Closets in 6 Easy Steps Using the KonMari Method," Popsugar, January 11, 2019, www.popsugar.com.

knew nothing about roof repair, but he was familiar with crowdfunding. He engaged the help of a local community volunteer organizer who helped coordinate the effort.

Shoulders found a local roofing contractor who offered to replace Paul's roof for the cost of materials only. This meant an $11,000 roof replacement job would be done for $5,500. Shoulders organized a fundraiser on the crowdfunding site GoFundMe and in one month raised enough money to fix the roof. When the project was completed, Shoulders wrote on the fundraising page: "We are a community, one body, and I will close with saying, Thank You All So Very Much for all you do in this great Orting Village!"[7]

Pets to People

While not everyone can raise funds to fix a roof, almost anyone can volunteer to help a neighbor. Elderly or ill neighbors might need help with simple tasks, such as walking their dog. Or, if you own a friendly dog or cooperative cat, you can take it around to visit seniors who live nearby. There are many emotional and physical benefits associated with what is called pet therapy. Studies show interacting with pets helps lower blood pressure and reduce anxiety and depression while bringing joy. This type of therapy can take place in a number of settings including a retirement home or a senior's home.

If you are unsure about your ability to handle your pet around new people—or if you do not have a pet—the group Pet Partners might be your answer. This organization, which has chapters throughout the United States and Canada, has run its Therapy Animal Program for more than forty years. The program caters to seniors, veterans with PTSD, patients in recovery, people with intellectual disabilities, and others who benefit from interactions with dogs and cats. Pet Partners also provides other therapy ani-

Not all volunteer projects involve dozens of people and extensive planning. Volunteering can be as simple as offering to walk the dog of a neighbor who cannot get out of the house to do that.

mals, including miniature horses, rabbits, macaws, and even rats. Those who register themselves and their pets with Pet Partners will have access to free online courses. They can also attend the Pet Partners Handler Course, which the website says is for "the human on the end of the leash."[8] The course teaches volunteers what to expect when working as a Pet Partners handler.

Trash It and Post It

If pet therapy is not on your agenda, you can make your neighborhood a better place by picking up trash. No matter where you live, you will likely find litter that needs to be placed in a trash can—fast food wrappers, water bottles, and all types of plastic junk are easy to find almost everywhere. You can start on your block and work your way out to local parks, beaches, and hiking trails. Inexpensive claw-type trash pickup tools, which can be found at hardware stores and online, can make it easier to pick up all sorts of objects. Other necessities include a pair of work gloves and a few large trash bags.

Most volunteers do what they do for altruistic (unselfish) reasons; they do not expect to receive awards or see their picture in the news. But most people like a pat on the back, or the modern equivalent, likes on social media. If you appreciate virtual kudos, you can participate in the #trashtag challenge promoted in 2019 by Facebook user Byron Román. "Here is a new #challenge for all you bored teens," Román wrote. "Take a photo of an area that needs some cleaning or maintenance, then take a photo after you have done something about it, and post it."[9] Román's post was accompanied by a "before" selfie in which he posed along a riverbank marred by a mess of ugly trash. The "after" selfie showed the results of Román's work: nine large garbage bags completely filled and tied next to a spotless area returned to its natural state.

Román is not a teenager; he is a fifty-three-year-old banker from Phoenix. But his #trashtag and #trashchallenge went viral among teens on social media; within days it was shared more than 323,000 times on Facebook. Within a week, hundreds of teens from the United States, Thailand, Germany, India, and elsewhere were sharing before-and-after pictures from their cleanup efforts along roadsides, riverbanks, and beaches. Some trash challenges included dozens of bags filled by ten or more people. Others' cleanups consisted of a single bag of junk the poster had picked up at a campsite. A tweet by a user named Megan summed up the satisfaction felt by many volunteers: "Usually I'm against doing good deeds just to post it online but in the case of #trashtag i am 100% for it, if that's what it takes. Good people are good."[10]

> "Usually I'm against doing good deeds just to post it online but in the case of #trashtag i am 100% for it, if that's what it takes. Good people are good."[10]
>
> —Megan, #trashtag volunteer

A Kid Changemaker

Caleb Oh wanted to be one of the good people who volunteer, but the eighth grader from Gambrills, Maryland, often suffered from debilitating migraine headaches. Sometimes he could not even attend school due to the painful throbbing in his head. In 2011, when Oh was in first grade, he was home with a headache reading the biography of Jane Goodall, the world's leading expert on chimpanzees. Inspired by Goodall's animal rights activism, he decided he would try to make a positive mark on the world. But Oh said he had trouble finding a place to fit in: "There was a fixed mindset that kids could not help. Most places require you to be at least 18 to volunteer."[11]

Oh was only six at the time, but he decided to launch his own initiative, Kid Changemakers. He recruited some of his friends, made one hundred bagged lunches, and donated them to a homeless shelter in nearby Annapolis. After the successful lunch donation, Oh found other ways to help. He launched a drive to collect toiletries and baby supplies for a local women's shelter.

Write a Letter to a Hero

Operation Gratitude sends care packages to deployed military personnel, first responders, wounded veterans, and others who serve—or have served—in the US Armed Forces or in fire, police, or emergency services. Some of the most cherished items in care packages are bundles of letters written by average folks who want to thank soldiers for their service to the country. Whatever your age or situation, you can write simple letters following the Operation Gratitude guidelines that follow. And don't be concerned if you don't get a response. Just know that your letter has given someone else a moment of pleasure.

- Start with a generic salutation, such as "Dear Hero" or "Dear Brave One."
- Express your thanks for their selfless service. . . .
- Avoid politics completely and religion in excess; however, saying you will pray for them is wonderful.
- Share a little about yourself: Families, Hobbies, Work, School, Pets, Travel, etc.
- Talk about your life and interests: Sports, Weather, Music, Movies, Food, Books, etc. . . .
- Children's Letters: Include first names only and do not include addresses (an adult's address can be used).
- Can't find the words? Consider drawing or painting a picture instead; please add a note to kids' drawings with their age.
- No glitter or confetti please!
- Please DO NOT put cards or letters in individual envelopes; all letters must go through an internal screening process and the envelopes slow the process down significantly.

Operation Gratitude, "Join Our Movement to Thank Every First Responder," 2020. www.operationgratitude.com.

Kid Changemakers also focused on foster children who often move from one foster family to another. The group supported a program called Backpacks of Love that provides foster kids with backpacks filled with clothes, toys, and toiletries.

In 2015, Oh applied for a grant to pay off money owed by kids in his school's lunch program. For this effort, he won the

Jane Goodall Roots & Shoots Service Grant Award. He says, "It was cool because I actually got to meet [Goodall]. My inspiration recognized me as someone good enough to be recognized. It all came full circle and makes me want to continue."[12] In 2019, Kid Changemakers was still going strong, and Oh won the Prudential Spirit of the Community Award. While the organization has had a far-reaching impact, Oh manages many of the group's activities from his home.

Kid Changemakers is a great example of a student volunteer who looked around, saw a local need, and took the initiative to help his neighbors.

Showing Gratitude to Soldiers

One of Oh's volunteer activities was aimed at helping military families living abroad. He learned that almost all troops are on tight budgets and many are stationed in countries where the dollar does not go far. But government-run grocery stores (commissaries) on military bases take coupons for discounts on food, cleaning products, and baby and pet supplies. Working at his kitchen table with a pair of scissors and mailers from grocery stores, he clipped coupons, bundled them up, and sent them to military families stationed overseas.

Anyone who wants to follow Oh's example can clip coupons and package them in zip-top bags. An organization called Support Our Troops, located in Daytona Beach, Florida, runs a program called Troopons that distributes the coupon packages to troops all over the world. More information is available on the Support Our Troops website.

Clipping coupons is a way student volunteers can help soldiers out financially. Those who wish to provide an emotional

Some teens volunteer to write letters to deployed troops, veterans, and wounded soldiers. The organization Operation Gratitude sends these letters along with care packages to thousands of soldiers every year.

boost can write letters to deployed troops, new recruits, veterans, and wounded soldiers and their caregivers. These cards and letters can be sent to Operation Gratitude to be included in the care packages the organization sends to thousands of soldiers every year. Other items in the care packages include food, clothing, books, toiletries, playing cards, personal care items, and other goods. But the operation's website says the letters of thanks from student volunteers are the most cherished items in each box. An airman named John, who was serving in the air force in the Middle East in 2019, expressed his gratitude:

> We're missing our families and friends but know our work here matters to the world and the safety of our nation. We received your care packages today and the . . . letters of love brought tears to peoples' eyes and knowing they're

remembered and cared for is a gift that is priceless to the soul. . . . Thank you so much, and if I could hug you all I would. It's an honor to serve the greatest people in the world, people like you![13]

While writing a letter to a stranger might seem difficult at first, no one is expecting perfect grammar or punctuation. As John's response shows, a simple expression of love and appreciation goes a long way for those suffering hardships while serving the nation. But if you do not feel comfortable expressing yourself in words, Operation Gratitude also takes handmade goods such as scarves, candles, and beanies. Drawings and paintings are also greatly appreciated. And many soldiers have kids of their own. They welcome artwork made with finger paint or crayons so even the youngest kids can join in.

Those who serve in the military are all volunteers themselves. They understand the importance of making a personal sacrifice for the greater good. While donating clothes or helping a neighbor rake leaves is not the same as serving overseas, you can make the world a better place starting today. German teenage diarist Anne Frank understood this even as she and her family hid from Nazis during World War II. As Frank wrote, "How wonderful that no one need wait a single moment to improve the world."[14]

"We received your care packages today and the . . . letters of love brought tears to peoples' eyes and knowing they're remembered and cared for is a gift that is priceless to the soul."[13]

—John, airman, US Air Force

CHAPTER TWO

Volunteer for a Day or Two

Civil rights leader Martin Luther King Jr. once said, "Everybody can be great, because everybody can serve."[15] In memory of King's service to the cause of racial equality, Congress created the Martin Luther King Jr. Day of Service in 1994. It is celebrated concurrently with Martin Luther King Jr. Day on the third Monday of every January.

Every year countless schools, universities, nonprofit organizations, and community groups organize Day of Service projects in all fifty states. Citizens deliver meals, fix up schools and community centers, build homes, provide services for veterans and their families, and collect food and clothing. Almost every town and city offers numerous opportunities to volunteer on the Day of Service. In Long Beach, California, in 2020 more than five hundred volunteers participated in twenty local service projects organized by Leadership Long Beach, the Port of Long Beach, and the City of Long Beach. Students worked alongside other volunteers to landscape a local park, decorate city trash barrels, paint a mural on the wall of a community service office, perform yard work for elderly and disabled people, and clean a local beach.

Promoters of the Day of Service say that the holiday is not a day off but a day on. Gwen Kieffer, an eighteen-year-old Wisconsin volunteer, explains: "Martin Luther King, Jr. did not want us to have a day off on this day, today should be a day where we give

> "Everybody can be great, because everybody can serve."[15]
>
> —Martin Luther King, Jr., civil rights leader

back to the community. It's really important that we are here today, serving the people who need it most, instead of sitting at home on a day off."[16] Kieffer spent her day of service in 2019 volunteering at the Eau Claire Community Table, serving food to around seventy-five low-income people.

Nine students in Pasadena, California, found another way to help out on the King National Day of Service in 2020. They spent nearly three hours cleaning up a local baseball field. The group picked up water bottles, caps, cigarette butts, and other garbage. As high school freshman Declan Swift says, "I just feel more connected to the parks in a way because I feel like I made them a bit better. It made me feel better about myself and what we were doing."[17]

Teen volunteers sort food at a Detroit, Michigan, food bank as part of a Martin Luther King Jr. Day of Service project. Other common Day of Service volunteer projects include delivering meals, fixing up schools, and collecting clothing for people in need.

The volunteers were members of a group called Lion's Heart 2023, which is a chapter of the Lion's Heart—Teen Volunteers and Leaders group. Parent Kristen Swift, a chaperone who helped found Lion's Heart 2023, explains the benefits: "We started this a couple of years ago just to get our boys out doing things, kind of off their computers, off their video games and doing things. They like it because they get to help people but they also get to be together, and so it's a double win for them."[18]

Fundraising Events

Volunteering can be hard work, educational, challenging, and gratifying—all at the same time. For busy people who have never volunteered, the rewards might not seem worth the time and effort required. If you are unsure you will be able to maintain a commitment to a cause—or measure up to a group's expectations—you can test the waters before jumping into the world of volunteering.

While the Day of Service is a nationally recognized volunteer opportunity, there are events held throughout the year that rely on short-term efforts by volunteers. You can help out for a day at a block party, art festival, marathon, beach cleanup, or another one-off event. Nonprofits that sponsor these activities are always eager to recruit volunteers, and helpers are not expected to have prior experience. Depending on the event, volunteers are used to register participants, sell merchandise, work at food booths, hand out water to runners, and perform other simple tasks. Those who participate interact with experienced organizers and get a peek behind the scenes. This is an excellent learning experience for those who wish to become committed volunteers. And most go home with swag such as water bottles, t-shirts, and tote bags.

"[Our boys like volunteering] because they get to help people but they also get to be together, and so it's a double win for them."[18]

—Kristen Swift, volunteer group chaperone

Volunteer at a Soup Kitchen

Volunteering at a soup kitchen for a day is not difficult if you know what to expect. Most operations are well run and staffed by experienced people who know how to train new volunteers. But there are a few health and safety precautions to consider if you want to serve food to those in need.

Dress appropriately: You will be on your feet all day; wear comfortable closed-toed shoes. Tie back your hair and be ready to wear a hair net. Do not wear rings, excessive jewelry, or revealing outfits.

Cleanliness is mandatory: shower before you arrive and wash your hands before, after, and during your shift, especially after using the bathroom.

Do not show up if you are sick: Many people who are served at soup kitchens have health issues and are vulnerable to germs and diseases. If you feel unwell, stay home.

Soup kitchen volunteers perform many menial tasks: They open boxes, clean and sort produce, peel potatoes, wash dishes, and clean tables and floors. Volunteers chop vegetables, cook, wipe down cutting boards and counters, compost food scraps, and take out the trash.

Be humble: Volunteering is an act of service. No one who visits a soup kitchen wants to be pitied or looked down upon. Smile, be compassionate, talk to guests, eat with them, and exchange stories. And do not expect thanks; sometimes people who are facing great challenges in their lives do not show appreciation.

Many national charity organizations hold events that are powered by volunteers. The Relay for Life is a fundraising event sponsored by the American Cancer Society. Over 4 million people participate in the relay, which takes place in over five thousand communities. During the twenty-four-hour event, team representatives conduct walking relays on tracks at high schools, colleges, city parks, fairgrounds, and elsewhere. Each relay team commits to raising money to meet a specific goal. The event is organized by the all-volunteer Relay Committee, which works year-round to sign up participants, book entertainment, and raise funds. Those who volunteer on the day of the event handle logistics such as setting up tents, booths, tables, chairs, stages, and other equipment—and tearing it all down when the event ends. Volunteers also hand out water and snacks to participants, put up banners, pick up trash, and help with other tasks.

Most other national and international organizations have big annual single-day events that rely on volunteers. The American Heart Association hosts the annual Heart Walk, which raises funds for research and education programs aimed at combating cardiovascular disease and stroke. The American Lung Association holds fundraisers to improve lung health and prevent lung disease through advocacy, education, and research. Events include the Lung Force Walks and Runs and the Fight For Air Climb, in which participants climb stairs to reach the top floors of skyscrapers.

The group Susan G. Komen (formerly known as the Susan G. Komen Breast Cancer Foundation) holds an annual More Than Pink Walk, which attracts thousands of participants in major cities. In the Marathon for the Cure, volunteers run or walk a full course of 26 miles (42 km) or a half course of 13 miles (21 km). Volunteers under age eighteen need to be accompanied by a parent or guardian.

Whatever the cause, student volunteers can participate in fundraising events by walking, running, or cycling or by helping with logistics. Volunteers might need to attend short training classes before the event.

Habitat for Humanity

Most national nonprofits hold their events on weekends, around the same time every year. But Habitat for Humanity builds houses for those in need at events held throughout the year. Most people know about Habitat for Humanity due to its most high-profile volunteer, Jimmy Carter, president of the United States from 1977 to 1981. In 2019, the ninety-five-year-old Carter was still at it, volunteering with his ninety-two-year-old wife, former first lady Rosalynn Carter. The Carters were in Nashville for the weeklong 36th Jimmy and Rosalynn Carter Work Project for Habitat for Humanity, which has built, renovated, or repaired more than forty-three hundred homes with more than ten thousand volunteers in fourteen countries.

Habitat for Humanity was founded in 1976. Jimmy Carter got involved in 1984 when he happened to come across a group of students struggling to complete a Habitat project in Brooklyn. Carter thought he needed to do something to help the students, and the Carter Work Project was born. Since that time, student volunteers have played a major role in the Work Project and other homebuilding events. The Habitat for Humanity Youth Programs website says the organization provides volunteer opportunities for ages five to forty. Visitors to the website can find projects in their community or find a local Habitat for Humanity campus chapter club run by students at high schools, colleges, and universities. Campus chapters partner with their local Habitat for Humanity chapter to provide volunteers for new home construction, rehabilitation, neighborhood revitalization, and office tasks.

In 2020, the Habitat for Humanity chapter club at Alexander High School in Atlanta, Georgia, decided to raise $90,000 to build a Habitat home for a local veteran. The group sold T-shirts, held bake sales, organized yard sales and raffles, and solicited donations from corporations. The enthusiasm exhibited by the students inspired adults to hold golf tournaments, poker nights, and other fundraisers to help the club meet its goals.

In addition to raising the funds, the students worked to build the home, which was one of eight Habitat for Humanity dwellings set aside for veterans. The volunteer effort took place over the course of nine Saturdays. Some volunteered for a single day; others were on the building site every Saturday. Habitat volunteer

Adults guide teen volunteers on a house-building project similar to the ones done by Habitat for Humanity. Youth volunteers help with fundraising, construction, rehabilitation, and office tasks.

Jimmy Haddle was amazed by the students' determination: "It's very unusual for a group of kids this young to do this. They're learning that it takes plain old hard work getting it done yourself."[19]

Habitat for Humanity accepts volunteers at all skill levels, and most have experiences similar to the students in Atlanta. Volunteers are not expected to bring anything for the day but a good attitude and a willingness to take on whatever job they are assigned. However, no one is required to take on a job that makes them uncomfortable. Helpers should dress for the weather: sunscreen and a hat in the summer and warm clothes when temperatures drop. Safety is the number-one priority; volunteers are asked to leave jewelry, loose-fitting clothes, and fashionable shoes at home.

Habitat helpers do not need prior construction experience, and questions are always welcome, as New Hampshire student volunteer Amanda Hardman explains:

When I first started with Habitat, I had never even swung a hammer, could barely lift anything, had no construction skills or knowledge, yet everyone welcomed me to the construction site. Don't be afraid to ask questions of the volunteer coordinator, site supervisor or even other volunteers. I have learned a lot by asking, and asking questions can save a lot of time. Don't be afraid to admit that you don't know something.[20]

Cleaning Up for the Environment

Habitat for Humanity homes are built with sustainable and recycled materials whenever possible. This helps the organization remain faithful to its Earth Day Resolution Challenge, which asks people to recycle, drive less, and conserve water and energy. Habitat for Humanity also calls on supporters to volunteer at a local event on Earth Day, which is celebrated every April 22.

When the first Earth Day was held in 1970, it was the largest demonstration in US history. More than 20 million people took part in Earth Day activities in thousands of communities across the

Connecting Kids with Lion's Heart

In 2004, Terry Corwin and her son Spencer were discussing volunteering in Santa Ana, California. They realized there was no organization or internet platform to connect kids with short-term volunteer opportunities. Terry and Spencer decided to create Lion's Heart—Teen Volunteers and Leaders to address the need.

Since its creation, Lion's Heart has expanded to include nearly ten thousand members in more than 250 chapters in thirty-one states. The organization connects sixth- through twelfth-grade students with age-appropriate volunteer opportunities. Visitors to the group's website (lionsheartservice.org) can type in their zip code and find volunteer openings in their communities ranging from a single-day commitment to longer terms of service.

The Lion's Heart app allows members to find opportunities, track service hours, connect with other student volunteers, and share their volunteer portfolios with the National Honor Society, colleges, scholarships, and job recruiters. Lion's Heart also produces the T.O.B.Y. Talk podcast dedicated to supporting teen volunteers. Many Lion's Heart volunteers have been recognized for their service through programs such as the President's Volunteer Service Award and the Congressional Award.

country. Classes were canceled at ten thousand public schools and on two thousand college campuses to celebrate the Earth. Students remained at the heart of Earth Day celebrations, which quickly grew into an international event. By 2019, an estimated 100 million people throughout the world had pledged to take steps to slow climate change and reduce environmental degradation.

Earth Day provides countless opportunities for volunteers who wish to serve for a day or two. The official Earth Day website (earthday.org) offers a signup section for local events. One of the most popular volunteer programs is an event called Great Global Cleanup. In 2019, millions of volunteers across the globe removed billions of pieces of trash from more than fifty-three hundred sites, including local neighborhoods, beaches, rivers, lakes, trails, and urban parks.

While the Great Global Cleanup is called the largest environmental volunteer event in the world, it has a close rival. World CleanUp Day, which coincides with National CleanUp Day in the United States, is held annually on the third Saturday of September. In 2019, World CleanUp Day attracted around 20 million volunteers in 179 countries. In the United States, around 2 million National CleanUp Day volunteers picked up 18 million pounds (8.1 million kg) of waste. The same day, around 1 million people who lived near oceans and lakes picked up 23 million pounds (10.4 million kg) of trash for the International Coastal Cleanup, sponsored by the nonprofit Ocean

Two young women take part in the International Coastal Cleanup at Erie Bluffs State Park in Pennsylvania. Events like this one draw millions of volunteers, including many teens, each year.

Conservancy. Hundreds of people in Flagler Beach, Florida, picked up trash that included PVC pipe and disintegrating sandbags that can be eaten by marine life. High school student volunteers included members of the Flagler County lacrosse team known as the Firehawks. Team member Lucas Wright comments, "We wanted to show that the Firehawks give back to the community. It's our home . . . and we want to give back."[21]

While making beaches a more beautiful place, Coastal Clean-up days provide valuable information for research. Every cigarette butt, piece of plastic, and snack wrapper is entered into an online database that provides information to public policy experts who enact policies that focus on waste issues.

Those individuals who are still eager to pick up trash after participating in their local cleanup day can volunteer for National Public Lands Day, which takes place the following week, on the fourth Saturday in September. As the name implies, National Public Lands Day is held on public lands at the federal, state, and local level. These lands include national parks, national forests, Bureau of Land Management sites, wetlands, wildlife preserves, and city and county parks. Admission fees to National Parks and other public lands are waived on National Public Lands Day. In 2019, over 156,000 people volunteered to grab shovels, rakes, and hoes and clean up trash at more than two thousand public land sites in forty-nine states, Washington, DC, and Puerto Rico. They also helped repair trails, plant gardens, and guide hikes. The monetary value of the services they performed was an estimated $16 million.

While pulling garbage from a riverbed is not most people's idea of fun, there is a sense of satisfaction when the mission is accomplished. And first-timers who volunteer for cleanup events, marathons, or other one-day events often discover that volunteering can be habit-forming. After meeting new people and working with them to achieve a common goal, fears of commitment often fade away, replaced by an eagerness to do more things for more people in the future.

CHAPTER THREE

Share Your Skills

University of New Mexico graduate student Trish Lopez saw first-hand how many senior citizens struggle with digital technology. In 2015, Lopez's mother grew increasingly frustrated and irritated while trying to work with her new computer: "She'd lose a password, she'd lose a document and then she didn't know some simple commands like Control Z that could undo everything she had just done. And so she would start all over again."[22] Lopez knew that most young people do not have such problems with technology. In 2016, she founded a nonprofit organization called Teeniors to connect tech-savvy students with older folks.

Teeniors is based on the idea that almost all kids today have been using cell phones and computers since they were little. But millions of seniors need help with new electronic devices. In 2020, there were 46 million people in the United States age sixty-five or older. While some understand the digital world, others struggle to adapt to the latest technology. A 2017 study by the Pew Research Center found four in ten seniors who owned smartphones had trouble using the devices. This increased their feelings of isolation, something that can have a negative effect on a person's health and well-being.

By 2020, Teeniors had served over three thousand senior citizens in New Mexico. A student volunteer helped demystify the cell phone experience for Camilla Dorsey, a seventy-six-year-old South Africa native who lives in New Mexico. According to Dorsey, "People would be ringing me and I didn't know how to answer [my phone]. I'd be crying and frustrated and feeling totally useless and old."[23] Dorsey returned to the store where she bought the phone, but the clerk did not understand why she was having problems. He unsympathetically told her a child could answer the phone. Seventeen-year-old Tess Reynolds showed Dorsey how to download WhatsApp, a text and voice messaging application, and how to use it. This allowed Dorsey to make free calls to her relatives in South Africa using her cell phone.

Dorsey is thrilled with her new skill and says she feels free again. The experience was also beneficial to Reynolds, who has a learning disability. Volunteering helps her feel compassion for seniors who might need extra time to learn something. "I know how it feels to be rushed," Reynolds said. "I want to make sure that doesn't happen."[24] And Reynolds credits her experience with Teeniors for giving her a new direction in life. She wants to work as a senior home health aide after graduation.

A Teeniors volunteer in Albuquerque, New Mexico, shows a senior citizen how to use her smartphone. Teeniors connects tech-savvy teens with senior citizens who need assistance using high-tech electronic devices.

According to Lopez, in sharing their own skills with others, many Teeniors volunteers have gained valuable life skills. They become better communicators, problem-solvers, public speakers, and coaches. And Lopez says the experience helped some overcome depression, anxiety, and struggles in their personal relationships: "Just the work of being a Teenior, for the small amount of hours they do it every month, has made an enormous impact on their lives."[25]

Connecting Through Music

Teeniors is one of many organizations around the country that pairs young people with senior citizens. Students who know how to play an instrument or sing can share the gift of music with appreciative older audiences who live in assisted living centers. Studies show that listening to music lowers stress and promotes relaxation. For older or disabled listeners, music can improve memory, encourage exercise, and evoke pleasing emotions. Musician Michael Levine was aware of the healing power of music when he founded Harmony Bridge in 2010. The group connects middle school and high school band students with older folks in their communities. Levine is from Minneapolis, and Harmony Bridge presented its first concerts in the Upper Midwest. Today the organization has expanded to include chapters in twenty-four communities in Minnesota, South Dakota, Arizona, New York, California, and even Finland. The group focuses on community outreach and personal growth and development for the students.

At a 2020 event in Rapid City, South Dakota, Harmony Bridge brought together students from five different middle schools in the area. The band kids rehearse with each other every few months and perform at senior facilities throughout the region. Haley Armstrong, director of music for Harmony Bridge, says students learn and grow from the experience:

> From the moment they meet they are so nervous; it's not just the musical side, but they don't know each other because they are from different schools, and then they start to play together and they realize there is this common language. And then they are really nervous again to talk to some of our senior citizens and then as soon as they have their first conversation, they realize these people have fascinating lives. . . . [The students] go from nervous to confident.[26]

Student musicians do not need to be part of a formal group like Harmony Bridge to serve in their community. Most hospitals recruit volunteer musicians to entertain patients, staff, and visitors. Hospital websites often have specific pages that list volunteer opportunities. Teenagers who play guitar, cello, violin, and

High school musicians perform for a group of elementary school kids. Some teen musicians also volunteer their time to perform for older audiences at assisted living centers.

piano perform regularly at the Henry Ford Hospital in West Bloom-field, Michigan. According to Director of Volunteer Services Linda Smith, "On spring break, they come in every day."[27]

Mathematics Masterminds

While some teens volunteer in hospitals or senior centers, others share their intellectual talents with their schoolmates. Sometimes the urge to help others is driven by the need to help one's self. Tulla Bee found herself in need of help when she began attending high school in Gulf Breeze, Florida, in 2016. As a freshman, Bee felt anxious and insecure, intimidated by the big, new school and the unfamiliar faces in the hallway. But unlike many students, Bee was not intimidated by mathematics. In fact, she was a math-ematics mastermind. She began offering math tutoring in the Gulf Breeze Library every Wednesday after school. Bee explains why she started her tutoring program: "This program is created to help students not only understand these problems, but also have a friendly face around the high school because I found high school absolutely terrifying."[28]

Bee's math classes were an instant hit with her classmates. The positive response motivated her to continue tutoring throughout her high school years. By 2019, she had helped over one hundred students. Along the way she recruited other math wizards at her high school who helped dozens of other students learn calculus, ge-ometry, and other subjects. Kellen McKenny was one of those volunteer tutors: "I like how she's reaching out into the community, and I like how she's asked me and a few other people to do it. . . . [Struggling students] don't have to go out and pay $50 per hour because we're giv-

"This [tutoring] program is created to help students not only understand these problems, but also have a friendly face around the high school because I found high school absolutely terrifying."[28]

—Tulla Bee, volunteer math tutor

ing away two hours every week of this math tutoring for them to come to."[29]

By the time she graduated high school, Bee was a member of the National Math Honor Society, Mu Alpha Theta, and had plans to study medicine in college. Bee says she will always remember the friendly faces of students she helped in the high school hallways that were once a source of her anxiety. Her story is a good reminder of how volunteering can be as beneficial to the volunteer as to the recipient.

"[Struggling students] don't have to go out and pay $50 per hour because we're giving away two hours every week of this math tutoring for them to come to."[29]

—Kellen McKenny, volunteer math tutor

Translating Through WhatsApp

While some students specialize in numbers, formulas, and calculations, others draw on their knowledge of foreign languages to help those in need. Jane Josefowicz is someone who understands the fears faced by non-English speakers in the United States. Josefowicz, who grew up in Providence, Rhode Island, learned to speak Arabic to communicate with relatives who had recently emigrated from Syria. In 2019, Josefowicz was a high school junior and a volunteer at the Refugee Dream Center (RDC) in Providence. An Arabic-speaking Syrian woman named Saadia approached Josefowicz with a pile of official letters she could not read because they were written in English. According to Josefowicz, "Some items were nearly a year old. What scared me most, though, were the letters about healthcare, Social Security, and the Rhode Island Works cash assistance program. . . . I knew they were important, and the letters might contain information that could not wait."[30]

Josefowicz realized this was a common problem for immigrants, especially women, who are often expected to perform tasks like enrolling children in school and applying for health insurance. Josefowicz decided to set up a program to connect

RDC clients with translators using WhatsApp. She explains how the program works:

> A person fluent in English with a working proficiency or fluency in another language such as Arabic, Kurundi, or Swahili, would be paired through WhatsApp with someone like Saadia, who wants help with understanding small things in English, like a letter. Each time they need something translated, they could send a picture to their translator, who would get back to them within a few days with either a voice message or a text . . . explaining what the document is and, if it is important, what to do with it.[31]

Josefowicz used her contacts at the RDC to recruit translators at local high schools and universities. She organized workshops to teach the translators about common government programs that they would likely be asked to explain to clients. She also provided contacts that connected clients with government case workers if necessary. To judge the success of the project, Josefowicz had RDC survey those who used the program to find out whether it was easy to use, offered quality translations, and reduced stress associated with mail. This information was used to improve the system. Josefowicz also integrated the program into the RDC's offerings so it would continue after she left Providence for college.

In 2020, Josefowicz was one of ten young people across the country to win a $5,000 grant from the United Way Worldwide. The microgrants are awarded to people ages thirteen to twenty-two who have innovative ideas for community service projects. Josefowicz used some of the grant money

"A person fluent in English with a working proficiency or fluency in another language . . . would be paired through WhatsApp with someone . . . who wants help with understanding small things in English."[31]

—Jane Josefowicz, volunteer translator

Music Cares

In 2018, junior Ayla Khan was a pianist and cellist in the school band at Herbert Henry Dow High School in Midland, Michigan. When she noticed an empty piano in the lobby of the MidMichigan Medical Center, she got an idea. Khan contacted her friend and fellow cellist Neil Janwani to help her form the Music Care Program. The goal was to bring local high school musicians to the MidMichigan Medical Center to play for families, patients, and hospital staff. "Music can bring people together, and that is important in the world today," Khan says.

Since it was formed in 2018, the Music Care Program has hosted twenty new acts, including solo performers, choirs, and quartets. Performers sign up for ten-minute slots online. Student volunteers get one hour of credit toward their volunteering goals for each time slot they perform. In 2019, Khan and Janwani were hoping to expand the program to include other hospitals and high schools in the region. As both prepared to head to college, they made plans to hand off leadership of the program to other volunteers. Janwani says his ultimate goal is to encourage the use of music for healing: "Whenever I played music it gave me a sense of calmness and grounding. Ayla and I know how powerful music can be and wanted to share it with everyone else at the hospital."

Quoted in Harsha Nahata, "MidMichigan Music Care Program Offers Soothing Escape for Patients, Families and Staff," Catalyst Midland, August 29, 2019. www.secondwavemedia.com.

to recruit volunteers who spoke other languages, including Haitian Creole and African languages such as Tigrinya, Kibembe, Somali, Swahili, and Kirundi. Her simple act of sharing her skills as a translator had grown into something much larger.

Online Opportunities

Volunteers who translate over WhatsApp are able to work from home. This aspect of volunteering grew in importance when the coronavirus pandemic struck in March 2020. Businesses, schools, parks, and government offices were shuttered as people were ordered to stay at home in order to stop the spread of the disease. With schools closed across the United States, many students were willing to offer their services while confined

An Illinois teen poses with her grandfather, whom she interviewed as part of the StoryCorps project. Thousands of teens have volunteered to interview older family members, whose stories are collected by the American Folklife Center.

at home. And there were many online opportunities that could be performed by those with basic skills like interviewing, operating basic recording software, or simply providing compassionate guidance to those in need. These opportunities do not require face-to-face contact with the public and can be performed by volunteers in good times and bad.

When the pandemic kept millions of people at home with their families, it offered a great opportunity for students to talk to relatives and learn more about their life stories. A project called StoryCorps searches for volunteers to record family histories and contribute them to the American Folklife Center at the Library of Congress. Some stories are broadcast on StoryCorps, a weekly NPR radio series.

StoryCorps is a nonprofit organization. It was launched in 2002 by radio producer David Isay, who wanted to record and share stories told by Americans from every walk of life in all fifty states. StoryCorps provides a free app that uploads recorded interviews to the American Folklife Center. The StoryCorps website features over 250,000 stories—many thousands uploaded by teenagers who recorded the recollections of older family members. Other stories are from teens who talk about their own lives. The stories cover every subject from happy childhood memories to struggles with sexual orientation or immigration status.

The StoryCorps website provides a list of questions to those who wish to contribute. Teens can find questions tailored to grand-parents, parents, siblings, teachers, and others. Interviewees can be asked to describe the happiest event in their lives, the sad-dest event, their earliest memories, their funniest family stories, or when they felt most alone. Volunteers who want to tell their own stories can pick the most relevant questions from the list. While StoryCorps encourages people to conduct interviews on Thanks-giving and other holidays, the app can help people pass the time anywhere families are gathered together. And the stories about today's joys and sorrows will have value long into the future; as StoryCorps managing director Colleen Ross says: "You're leaving a message in a bottle for your great-great-grandchildren."[32]

Be Someone's Voice or Eyes

While some are recording their own family stories for posterity, there is also a need to preserve stories that were written long ago. The LibriVox project is dedicated to making millions of books available in audio format for free on the internet. These books are in the public domain, meaning they are no longer under copyright because they were written before 1923. Titles include classics like *War and Peace* by Leo Tolstoy and *Anne of Green Gables* by Lucy Maude Montgomery. LibriVox relies on volunteers to read the books aloud in all languages using common software programs like Audacity and GarageBand. Prior experience is not necessary, and there are no age restrictions. The LibriVox app and website explain how the process works.

LibriVox volunteers read short works of poetry, chapters from long texts, and entire books. The process is educational for readers and enjoyable for listeners. Audiobooks are also vital to those who have vision problems. Another way to help people who have trouble seeing is through the app Be My Eyes, which connects volunteers with people with vision loss.

After signing up with Be My Eyes, volunteers are contacted through a live video call by people who need visual help. Sighted volunteers communicate with clients who point their phone cameras at things they cannot see. They might need help identifying food items, street signs, and units of money, or reading product labels, receipts, or cooking instructions. Sometimes clients need help cooking meals, operating vending machines, or navigating their surroundings.

Be My Eyes was launched in 2015. By 2020, there were around 2 million volunteers available to aid about one hundred thousand visually impaired users. Help is offered in around twenty-five languages. Be My Eyes volunteers might only receive one or two calls a year, and they only need to answer the phone if they wish to. But as Be My Eyes chief executive Christian Erfurt says, "Sometimes it's a quick fix, other times it's a longer conversation of 'what's life like where you are.' . . . That reminds us that we're not that different, and the gap between 'us and them' is minimized."[33]

Play a Game, Feed the World

While you might not qualify to be a translator or tutor, you can help feed a hungry world if you are good at trivia. That is the idea behind the quiz game Freerice, released by the United Nations' World Food Programme (WFP). The game can be played on a free app or on a desktop computer, and gameplay is easy. Multiple-choice questions appear on the screen. When a player picks the correct answer, an advertisement is shown. In exchange for this service, the advertiser pays the WFP a small sum of money, enough to purchase around ten grains of rice. While it might not sound like much, approximately 620,000 people play Freerice every month, and the program has raised over $1.4 million. In countries where rice is a staple, Freerice provides around 400 grams (14 oz) of rice per person, per day.

Freerice is available in multiple languages and offers games that focus on various educational categories including climate change, healthy eating, vocabulary, and famous paintings. Freerice can be played by groups. Mandy A. Yang in Woodbridge, California, describes her experience:

> In middle school, my teacher introduced the website to us as an extra credit assignment. After we donated ten thousand grains of rice—or answered one thousand geography and humanities questions—we would receive a certain number of extra credit points. . . . Everybody in my class really enjoyed earning extra credit—and helping assist in the effort to end world hunger was a bonus.

Mandy A. Yang, "Nonprofit Spotlight: Freerice," Lion's Heart, July 16, 2019. https://lionsheartservice.wordpress.com.

Volunteering is always about minimizing the difference between us and them, as Erfurt puts it. And by offering your skills, talents, or even a pair of eyes, you can help make the world better for those who are struggling with language, learning, hearing, or seeing. Whether you are sitting at home with nothing to do, or you are searching for a way to make the world a better place, you might find volunteering opportunities by simply looking in the mirror. You will realize that the skills you were born with—and often take for granted—can be very useful to others.

CHAPTER FOUR

Committing to a Cause

The beauty of volunteering is that you can be as dedicated as you want to be. If you have time constraints, you can volunteer for a day or two. If you are moved to throw yourself into a worthy cause, you can make a strong commitment that might require you to step outside your comfort zone to express your ideals. In 2019, students Hannah Koch and Katie Campbell sacrificed their personal comfort and went beyond the minimum volunteer hours required to complete their senior project at Central Mountain High, in Clinton County, Pennsylvania. Koch and Campbell are both animal lovers, so they decided to volunteer at a local animal shelter. But they wanted to do more. The students wanted to draw attention to the plight of dogs that are locked in cages most of the day. According to Koch, "I just felt like I needed to do something bigger than just do my hours and get it done with, so I texted [Campbell] one morning and asked 'are you crazy enough to stay in a kennel with me.'"[34] Campbell said yes. The duo soon found themselves organizing an event in which they would spend twenty-four hours in the shelter dog kennels.

Koch and Campbell ate and used the restroom at the same time as the dogs. And they were only allowed outside if a shelter volunteer took them for a walk. The experience was an emotional one for Koch and Campbell, who spent an entire day and night surrounded by barking dogs, unable to leave. "To be in this one spot and just hope that somebody comes by to see, it's kind of hard to believe that this is what a dog sees,"[35] Koch says.

While few teens are committed enough to animal welfare to spend a night in a cage, many choose to volunteer at animal shelters on a regular basis. Organizations that operate shelters prefer volunteers who are willing to make a long-term commitment, rather than those who drop in for a day or two. In Arlington, Virginia, the Lucky Dog Animal Rescue organization (which also rescues lucky cats) relies on volunteers under the age of eighteen to walk dogs, play with cats, and help at weekly adoption events. Student volunteers draw attention to the cause by bringing dogs and cats into schools where they teach kids about the importance of rescue operations. Helpers have dog- or cat-themed birthday parties in which guests bring treats or make toys that can be donated to the shelter. Volunteers are encouraged to host donation drives, bake sales, and dog washes to raise awareness and money for the shelter. Lucky Dog volunteers over the age of fifteen help in the office with administrative tasks and data entry, train younger volunteers, and assist at adoption events.

A teen volunteer cares for a kitten at a New York City animal shelter. Volunteer work in one setting sometimes leads to other volunteer opportunities or even inspires a new idea.

Shelters like Lucky Dog can be found in every state, and all of them rely on public support. Long-term, experienced volunteers help these organizations focus on their main mission: rescuing animals and finding them forever homes. Matthew Bershadker, CEO of the American Society for the Prevention of Cruelty to Animals (ASPCA), explains: "Helping vulnerable animals and keeping pets in safe and loving homes requires a commitment from all of us—advocates, pet owners, shelters, leaders, and entire communities. When we work together under a common cause, we're both saving lives and elevating our society."[36]

Teens Counseling Teens

There are many important causes that compete for the public's attention, but one of the most pressing issues is teen suicide. While this problem does not always make headlines, psychologists point out that suicide is the most common cause of death for people between the ages of fifteen and thirty-four. Some of the most committed teen volunteers work at one of the hardest jobs imaginable, counseling their peers about anxiety, depression, grief, and suicidal thoughts. These volunteer counselors work at organizations that operate crisis hotlines where they take calls, texts, and emails from troubled kids and young adults who are contemplating suicide.

According to a study by the youth research organization Child Trends, nearly one in five teenagers had serious thoughts about suicide in 2017. Seven percent attempted suicide. While there are no confirmed reasons for this trend, some blame digital technology. Child psychologist Mary Fristad describes social media as "another realm of things to worry about, pressure to build your

Peer-to-Peer Counseling

Research shows that teenagers facing emotional challenges relate better to counselors who are their own age. Cheryl Eskin, who is a program director for the Los Angeles peer counseling service Teen Line, explains why teen volunteers are qualified to help people their own age:

> There is something about talking to someone who gets it, who knows your little lingo on text or just can say, 'Oh, yeah, I'm in high school, too.' I think just the cultural references are the same. It's not uncommon for a call that's been really heavy to start talking about the music they both like or their favorite Netflix shows. It's also just less intimidating to talk to a peer than an adult.
>
> To our knowledge, we've never had someone die by suicide after talking to us. I think our teens are really good at de-escalating the crisis of people calling us who are really upset. It doesn't mean that the next night, that they're not struggling, but hopefully, we've started the conversation and gotten them to maybe get help in their own lives.

Quoted in "Youth, for Youth," YR, March 11, 2020. https://yr.media/news/in-los-angeles-a-crisis-hotline-by-youth-for-youth.

brand, sharing too much and making unrealistic comparisons to other kids . . . being constantly on the phone and not engaging in face-to-face interactions."[37]

Social media is one of several root causes for depression and suicidal thoughts. But peer support—or help from other teens—is effective in helping young people who suffer from mental health problems. Seventeen-year-old Katarina Grealish is a crisis intervention specialist who talks to troubled callers at the YouthLine in Portland, Oregon. Grealish explains why peer-to-peer counseling is important: "Teenagers have a lot of black and white thinking. And so it can be really hard to have an adult, who has more of the gray area thinking, point out the gray area."[38]

All volunteers at YouthLine are between the ages of fifteen and twenty. Each volunteer commits to working one three-and-a-half-hour shift per week for at least one year. Many put in for extra shifts and volunteer at the organization for several years. To volunteer at YouthLine, counselors must first complete a three-hour orientation session and undergo sixty-three hours of training with psychologists who listen in on calls and review texts, chats, and emails sent to the hotline. The experts share suggestions and ideas when necessary.

Hotline volunteers try to encourage callers to speak with a trusted adult such as a parent, counselor, or neighbor. If a caller has been abused or is in immediate danger, the YouthLine volunteer is required to call child protective services or the police. However, the large majority of callers do not require emergency services; most simply want to talk to a caring person about everyday teenage troubles, including breakups, bullying, bad grades, and parental problems. (About one-quarter of the YouthLine calls are from the Portland area, while the rest come from teens living elsewhere in the United States.)

"I started volunteering at YouthLine because I felt like a lot of my friends were coming to me with these really intense issues and I felt powerless to help them."[39]

—Katarina Grealish, teen crisis intervention specialist

Volunteering at a hotline does not require any special talents, just empathy and the ability to listen and relate to callers. And volunteers find that by helping others, they build their own confidence. As Grealish explains, "I started volunteering at YouthLine because I felt like a lot of my friends were coming to me with these really intense issues and I felt powerless to help them."[39] YouthLine armed Grealish with the experience she needed to assist her friends. Grealish and other YouthLine volunteers continue their outreach efforts when they are not taking calls and texts. They serve as mentors to troubled kids, attend conferences, and

A Teen Line volunteer speaks at an event honoring the organization's volunteer teen counselors. These young people answer hotline calls, texts, and emails from troubled youth.

speak to the media to raise public awareness about teen mental health issues.

YouthLine is one of five youth suicide intervention services in the United States. In Los Angeles, the Teen Line accepts volunteers who are at least fourteen years old. Cheryl Eskin, program director at Teen Line, describes the process: "Each training is 65 hours, and [volunteers] have to commit to coming into all the trainings. So it's a huge commitment, but they actually love training. It becomes a lot like group therapy in some ways. During that time, they also do 15 practice role-plays, which mock calls or texts about a specific subject."[40]

Volunteers from Teen Line, YouthLine, and similar organizations speak to a

> "Each training is 65 hours, and [volunteers] have to commit to coming into all the trainings. So it's a huge commitment, but they actually love training."[40]
>
> —Cheryl Eskin, Teen Line program director

combined fifty thousand people annually. Those who work with these groups have monthly teleconferences to share their experiences and best solutions with other volunteers. And in 2019, teen volunteers were honored at a conference held by the American Association of Suicidology in Denver. The students held a question-and-answer session to explain how adult counselors could better connect with young people. However, psychologist Wendy Farmer, who attended the conference, was initially concerned for the young volunteers. She felt they were at risk of getting what is called vicarious trauma, a condition that affects those who counsel people experiencing pain, fear, and terror. These traumatic emotions can be transferred to volunteers who are not properly trained.

Farmer's apprehension led her to travel to Portland to work side-by-side with YouthLine volunteers. Farmer says she was "really blown away"[41] by how smart the volunteers were—and how effective they were in serving their peers. She said that the work seemed beneficial to the volunteers; it helped them build their emotional resilience rather than dragging them down with vicarious trauma. And the experience changed Farmer's view on whether teens should volunteer on crisis lines: "I don't know why we haven't embraced the idea that young people can help young people."[42]

Committing to a Healthier Planet

A long-term commitment to a crisis hotline might not be for everyone. But volunteers who want to draw attention to an important cause can find plenty of opportunities working for environmental organizations. A quick Google search will lead to mainstream organizations, smaller local groups, and those that focus on specific aspects of the environment such as oceans or endangered species. Most organization websites have signup pages for volunteers. And some environmental groups are entirely composed of volunteers in their teens and early twenties. One such organization, the Sunrise Movement, is the driving force behind the

Boot Camp for the Environment

The Sunrise Movement is an environmental organization made up of teens and twenty-somethings who are committed to slowing climate change. Every summer the group holds a weeklong boot camp to teach activists how to motivate others to join the movement. Around seventy-five volunteers from all walks of life attend the event, which has been held at a summer camp in Pennsylvania and a retreat center in New York.

The Sunrise Movement boot camp has been called a cross between a hippie summer camp and a high school pep rally. Participants sing songs, perform skits, and cheer each other on. Attendees learn team-building exercises, member-recruiting techniques, and protest planning. An important aspect of training focuses on teaching volunteers how to persuade others to join the movement by canvassing, or knocking on doors. An unnamed blogger on the Sunrise Movement website describes the training:

> [On the sixth day of boot camp] we dug into some hard canvassing skills, as in how we might talk to people at their doors and in our community to hear about challenges they're facing in their neighborhoods, share [info] with them about Sunrise and our plan to stop climate change, and invite them to join our movement. We role-played and practiced with one another—talking to strangers can be intimidating! But we know that unless thousands more join our movement, we won't have the power to stop the corruption of our politics and protect our generation's future.

"Sunrise Semester Book Camp: Days 5–7," Sunrise Movement, June 13, 2018. https://medium.com/sunrisemvmt /sunrise-semester-bootcamp-days-5-7-eae4e1987b8a.

Green New Deal. This proposed federal legislation is aimed at addressing climate change and economic inequality.

The Sunrise Movement was founded in 2015 by two twenty-one-year-old community organizers, Sara Blazevic and Varshini Prakash. The founders wanted to draw attention to climate change and lobby politicians to address the issue as an urgent crisis. In 2018, the Sunrise Movement raised enough funds to rent homes, known as movement houses, in cities across the country. Each movement house served as headquarters where committed student volunteers gathered to organize campaigns for political candidates who supported their cause. Volunteers held fundraisers, wrote articles, and knocked on doors to drum up support for candidates who supported the Green New Deal.

When the midterm congressional elections were held in 2018, half of the twenty candidates supported by the Sunrise Movement won their races. One of those candidates, Alexandria Ocasio-Cortez from Brooklyn, New York, introduced Green New Deal legislation in Congress. This would not have happened without the efforts of the committed environmental volunteers. By 2019, the Green New Deal was receiving widespread public attention, as journalist Sam Adler-Bell writes: "[The Sunrise Movement's] ambitious demand for a 'Green New Deal' . . . was on the lips of every congressional staffer, cable news reporter, and progressive candidate for president in the country. . . . Longtime climate wonks and advocates [were astonished] at the sudden ubiquity of the Green New Deal."[43]

While the Green New Deal faced an uphill political battle in Congress, the Sunrise Movement expanded its presence. The group opened movement houses in eighty cities and founded chapters in more than 150 other locations. Each movement house is used as a hub that is run by a leader who has trained in a weeklong Sunrise Movement boot camp. Hub leaders recruit student volunteers who choose what issues to highlight in their communities and which candidates to support in local elections. Nineteen-year-old Emily LaShelle, who attended the boot camp in 2019, explains the importance of training people to get involved for the long term: "When we were taught about the civil rights movement as kids, it was told to us as if a few big marches just happened and then the laws changed. . . . But there was so much more work and effort by activists behind the scenes. And that's the kind of work we're teaching people to be involved in for this movement."[44]

Sunrise Movement cofounder Varshini Prakash talks about the Green New Deal during a 2019 conference in Washington, DC. This group, with its many teen volunteers, is involved in issues relating to climate change.

Like the civil rights activists of an earlier generation, students who join the Sunrise Movement are willing to take personal risks to draw attention to their cause. In 2020, the Sunrise Movement organized a headline-grabbing demonstration on the Martin Luther King Jr. Day of Service. Over 150 middle and high school students from all fifty states assembled at the US Capitol in Washington, DC, to hold a teach-in. This event was meant to educate senators about the importance of the Green New Deal. Twenty teens were arrested inside the building after senators refused to meet with them. Seventeen-year-old John Paul Mejia of Miami explains why he is committed to the movement: "Instead of leaving our classrooms for our day off, we are bringing our classroom to the capitol because our government is failing to protect our generation. . . . The Green New Deal is about making sure that my generation . . . has basic rights to a safe climate, clean air and water, and a good job making our country a better place."[45]

Before the teach-in, Sunrise Movement volunteers held a two-day middle and high school summit where students attended workshops and training sessions put on by other students. At these sessions, students studied social movements from the past and present, including the 1960s civil rights movement and the 2018 #NeverAgain gun control effort. Volunteers learned to present the group's environmental message in personal terms, talking to officials about how their own lives were affected by climate change. Additionally, protesters were taught how to take direct, nonviolent action to participate in the protest at the capitol. Sunrise Movement's board member Becca Rast explains: "Young people are the most politically liberated force in our country right now. . . . We have less to lose than any other generation, and everything to gain. We can be radical. We can be visionary."[46]

Agents of Change

Students can be agents of change by committing to an environmental group, a youth hotline, an animal shelter, or any other organization that inspires them. Whatever the cause, committed volunteers use time-honored techniques to amplify their message. Like volunteers in the Sunrise Movement, they research issues, develop strategies, raise money, circulate petitions, speak to media outlets, lobby politicians, and publicize events on social media.

According to a 2017 report by the National Survey of Student Engagement (NSSE), one in eight college freshmen said they had committed themselves to a worthy cause in high school. The report says the volunteers seemed to have broader life skills than their nonactivist peers. They interacted more often with people of different racial and religious backgrounds, gender orientations, and political views. While making the world a better place, student volunteers develop critical thinking skills and a devotion to their communities that often set the stage for a lifelong love of civic engagement. Advocating for a cause can be hard work. But it might feel better to make good things happen, rather than simply letting things happen to you.

CHAPTER FIVE

Create Your Own Project

In December 2019, seventeen-year-old Seattle resident Avi Schiff-mann was reading the news when he saw that there was a horrific health crisis happening far from his home. A rapidly spreading virus had killed around one thousand people in Wuhan, China. At the time, few people outside China had heard of the coronavirus or COVID-19, the disease caused by the virus. And few Americans showed interest in what seemed to be a localized health problem. But as Schiffmann explains, he was moved to create a website called nCoV2019.live: "I saw this on the news . . . and I noticed that it was really hard just to find the information. And there was a lot of just misinformation spreading. So I decided it would be kind of cool to create a website and just kind of make it like a central hub of information."[47]

By February 2020, the coronavirus had become a worldwide pandemic that sickened and killed thousands of people. As officials in the United States, Italy, and elsewhere struggled to slow the spread of the disease, Schiffmann's website went viral. By March 2020, it had become a vital resource for more than 40 million people, including concerned citizens, journalists, doctors, health experts, and government officials.

The site nCoV2019.live breaks down pandemic statistics into simple graphics and easy-to-read statistics divided by state, nation, and continent. Schiffmann's website reports the total number of confirmed COVID-19 cases and the number of people killed by the virus. After receiving emails that said the site was too negative and depressing, Schiffman added a new tracker to give people hope. It lists the number of people who had COVID-19 and recovered.

Schiffmann's website automatically updates every minute using a process called web scraping. This process instantly gathers virus information from health departments including the World Health Organization, the Centers for Disease Control and Prevention, and other official news sources throughout the world. Although Schiffmann learned to code when he was seven, he never really learned web development. He says, "A lot of it was, you know, just kind of learning as I went along. I mean, you can learn like anything online. . . . If I had a question, I didn't know how to do a certain thing, I just went on Google and searched it up, figured out how to do it and eventually got it to work."[48]

Schiffmann had a lot more time to work on the website in mid-March. The pandemic forced the closure of all schools across the country, including Mercer Island High School, where he was

"If I had a question, I didn't know how to do a certain thing, I just went on Google and searched it up, figured out how to do it and eventually got it to work."[48]

—Avi Schiffmann, website creator

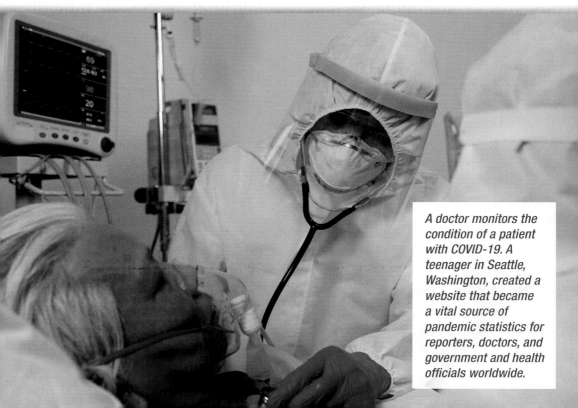

A doctor monitors the condition of a patient with COVID-19. A teenager in Seattle, Washington, created a website that became a vital source of pandemic statistics for reporters, doctors, and government and health officials worldwide.

a senior. With school closed, Schiffmann enlisted a few of his friends to work remotely with him to help with the hundreds of daily emails he received for bug fixes and other issues. And while Schiffmann's project was a volunteer effort, he added a "Buy Me a Coffee" button which allowed visitors to support his work by donating three or more dollars to the project.

Schiffmann, who was spending all of his free time on the website, shares this message with other students who might want to start their own projects: "You can combine technology and global health together to just make something really neat. And I hope it inspires a lot of people to, you know, maybe learn programming and make their own tracker in the future, because the more information that's easily accessible, the better."[49]

Setting Records

Most people do not have the technical knowledge needed to launch a vital website during a time of crisis. But thousands of students with a passion for a cause have created successful volunteer projects on their own. Most begin with a simple idea. Oftentimes, a young person will be moved to start a nonprofit organization after witnessing a troublesome event.

In 2015, eleven-year-old Kenan Pala was sparked to action when he saw two incidents that made him question people's values. Pala was jogging on a San Diego beach when he witnessed a sick baby seal lying in the sand, surrounded by beachgoers. While some were on their phones calling animal rescue services, others wrapped the seal in beach towels to provide comfort. On the way home, Pala saw a homeless person who was sick and in need of help. But the public reaction was completely different. According to Pala, "[People] just drove by, walked by, biked by. . . . They treated him like he was invisible."[50] The difference in responses disturbed Pala. When he got home, he began researching the issue of homelessness in San Diego. Pala found out that his hometown ranked number four in American cities

Outreach to Athletes and Officials

When Adom Appiah decided to host the Ball4Good Celebrity Basketball Game at his middle school in Spartanburg, South Carolina, he asked basketball star Anthony Ianni to participate. As Appiah learned, inviting well-known athletes to participate in an event can help make it a success. The Youth Service America organization offers the following guidelines for teens who wish to invite athletes, celebrities, public officials, and business leaders to a charity event:

> People's schedules fill up quickly! You should start reaching out to influential community leaders at least 1 month out from the date of your event, but you should send them information about your project and how you would like them to get involved as early as you can. . . .

> Make sure you are asking the right person for what you want. Some public officials may have multiple staff members that handle different kinds of requests. The best way to find out who to talk to is to call their office . . . and ask for the contact information for the best person in the office to handle your request. . . .

> Ask the person to RSVP by a specific date so you can include their support in your future press releases.

> Be ready with multiple options of how they can get involved. Only ask for one or two to start with, but if they say that cannot do one of them, have another option ready. . . .

> After your project, be sure to thank and recognize the influential community leaders who supported your project.

Youth Service America, "MLK Day of Service," 2020. http://leadasap.ysa.org.

with the highest number of homeless people. As Pala later recalled: "From what I had seen, people were not aware of this issue or aware of the impacts it has on our community and just how terrible of a thing it is. So that's when I thought, what can I do to raise awareness for homelessness, and how can I raise awareness for homelessness in a creative way that benefits [the homeless] as well?"[51]

In 2016, Pala came up with a unique idea to raise awareness about the issue. As a fan of the Guinness World Records website, Pala decided to draw attention to homelessness by trying to set a world record. He led a team of students on a food drive to collect new, unopened cereal boxes that were either red or blue. The group collected 3,924 boxes and assembled them into a giant heart-shaped mosaic on the floor of the gym at Francis Parker Middle School. The project attracted widespread media attention and broke the Guinness World Record for largest mosaic created with cardboard boxes. The cereal was later donated to a local food bank.

Inspired by the success of the project, Pala launched a local nonprofit, Kids4Community, to encourage kids ages five and up to get involved in charitable projects. Kids4Community projects include food and clothing drives, sandwich-making for the homeless, and serving dinner at shelters. Once a month, child and teenage volunteers in San Diego assemble two thousand canvas "Bags of Hope"—hygiene kits for homeless people that contain shampoo, body wash, toothpaste, toothbrushes, toys, and other essentials.

Pala received national recognition for his efforts. In 2017, he was named one of the top ten youth volunteers in the country by the Prudential Spirit of Community Awards, and in 2018 the mayor of San Diego declared January 23 "Kenan Pala Day" in the city. By 2019, Kids4Community had raised more than half a million dollars for homeless initiatives.

Charity Basketball

Adom Appiah, of Spartanburg, South Carolina, is another student who came up with a creative way to raise money for children in need. Appiah was in seventh grade in 2016 when his history teacher, Kelsea Turner, gave the class an assignment. Students

South Carolina student Adom Appiah (pictured at the 2018 Scripps National Spelling Bee) devised a creative way to raise money for children in need. His Ball4Good Celebrity Basketball Game attracted a sold-out crowd.

would dedicate one period per week to work on a yearlong service project. Turner explains, "It requires [students] to wonder, dream, set deadlines, find mentors and focus their energy outside of themselves. Their grade does not depend on the success of the project, and they are encouraged to embrace the lessons that come from their failures."[52]

Appiah was well acquainted with volunteering. He had worked with his parents as they organized book drives and backpack giveaways and served food to the hungry. He knew that most charities were in a constant scramble for money. In addition to volunteering, Appiah loved sports. He was also the Upstate Regional Spelling Bee champion who took part in the

Delivering Groceries in a Crisis

When the coronavirus pandemic closed schools in Santa Clarita, California, in March 2020, high school seniors Zoe Monterola and Eric Luo were not in the mood to sit around playing video games. The duo created Six Feet Supplies to deliver groceries to older people who were afraid to go out in public because they were at a higher risk of contracting the illness. The group took its name from the physical distancing measures put in place by officials; people were told to stay 6 feet (1.8 m) away from one another to avoid contracting the disease.

Six Feet Supplies quickly attracted thirty-seven volunteers who took orders by phone, text, or email and delivered goods to the front doors of those in need. Recipients left envelopes with cash or paid through a mobile payment service. (Volunteers wore surgical masks and gloves to protect themselves from infection.) Within a week of its launch, Six Feet Supplies was serving more than a dozen clients every day. User Leena Bhakri describes her experience with the service: "The delivery boy was so fabulous. He had a mask, but I could see him smiling though his eyes. I almost cried."

After Six Feet Supplies made national news, the group received requests from like-minded high school volunteers across the country. Luo and Monterola created a toolkit to help them set up their own supply services. A crisis often brings out the best in people and the students who volunteered at Six Feet Supplies certainly proved that point.

Quoted in Paul Bond, "Meet the California Teens Who Turned Shopping for Their Vulnerable Neighbors into a Full-Time Occupation," *Newsweek*, April 2, 2020. www.newsweek.com.

Scripps National Spelling Bee. In 2017, while he was training for his second spelling bee, Appiah took time out to organize the Ball4Good Celebrity Basketball Game. Appiah organized student volunteers who worked to make the charity basketball game a success. As Turner explains, "Once the momentum began to build, Adom's inspiration to make his project successful became palpable. He recruited some of his classmates to volunteer at his first event and it seemed to be really rewarding for him to see the community invested in coming together for the benefit of others."[53]

The charity basketball game attracted a sold-out crowd of more than eight hundred to the gym at Spartanburg Day School where Appiah was a student. After raising nearly $10,000 for local charities that help kids in need, Appiah set up the nonprofit organization Ball4Good. Appiah recruited adults, including Turner, his parents, and others to serve on the nonprofit's board of directors. They helped Appiah with the complex legalities required to set up a tax-exempt nonprofit organization. As Ball4Good grew, the board of directors expanded to include people who were familiar with grant applications and distribution of charity funds.

By 2020, Ball4Good had raised over $70,000 with its annual charity basketball game. The money has gone to the Boys and Girls Club, the Children's Advocacy Center, the Project Hope Foundation, and other charities. Celebrity athletes who have participated include Zion Williamson of the NBA's New Orleans Pelicans, former NFL player Landon Cohen, and WNBA all-star Andrea Stinson. In 2019, the roster included former Michigan State University basketball player Anthony Ianni, the first athlete with autism to play Division I basketball.

As if starting his own nonprofit and competing in two spelling bees were not enough, Appiah also became an author. In 2017, he wrote *Kids Can Change the World: A Middle Schooler's Guide for Turning Passion into Progress*. He donates 50 percent of the profits from the book to organizations that serve children. Appiah also speaks at schools and community events where he encourages kids to give back to their communities. In 2019, he was awarded $10,000 by the Gloria Barron Prize for Young Heroes. When Appiah spoke at the opening ceremony of the National Spelling Bee in 2018, he explained his core values: "The most memorable part of Ball4Good is the opportunity to play with and talk to other kids about the importance of working hard. I encourage them to tap into their passion and talents and use them for good."[54] Unfortunately, Appiah did not

> "I encourage [kids] to tap into their passion and talents and use them for good."[54]
>
> —Adom Appiah, founder of Ball4Good

win the 2018 spelling bee. His second book, *Bouncing Back from Failure: By a Kid for Kids*, is about that experience.

From Instagram to Activism

Appiah established his nonprofit organization using time-honored techniques. When he decided to set up Ball4Good, he used money he had received for his thirteenth birthday as seed money to fund the cause. He picked a name, set up a website, and established a presence on social media. Appiah branded the organization with hashtags, graphic emblems called logos, and short phrases called taglines—all of which worked together to create a memorable public image for his group.

Social media also provided a launching pad for fourteen-year-old Winter BreeAnne in 2016. BreeAnne started a group called Black Is Lit on Instagram to share positive stories about black people in her community. She felt that the group was needed because a lot of the stories concerning young black men in the media were not positive, or even factual. BreeAnne describes the Black Is Lit as "a platform to uplift the positive everyday stories of Black people in our communities."[55]

Black Is Lit attracted thousands of followers and transformed into a national movement. BreeAnne used her platform to reach out to communities through visits to elementary schools where she informed students about the importance of youth politics and voting.

The popularity of Black Is Lit led BreeAnne to become involved in a wider range of issues. She was invited to the Congressional Black Caucus annual legislative conference in Washington, DC, in 2017. The event addresses critical issues facing minority communities and provides leadership opportunities for young people. At the conference, BreeAnne was recruited by the co-chairs of the Women's March to lead the Women's March Youth Empower group. The Women's March is an advocacy group that works to protect women's rights. In 2018, BreeAnne organized the Youth Empower #PowerToThePolls campaign to educate and register young voters across the country. While BreeAnne was not old enough to vote at the time, she urged her social media followers to get involved in any way they could, such as ensuring family members were registered to vote.

In addition to voting rights, BreeAnne dedicated time to ending gun violence. She was one of the chief organizers of the #ENOUGH: National Student Walkout in March 2018. The walkout took place exactly one month after the deadly shooting that killed seventeen students at Marjory Stoneman Douglas High School in Parkland, Florida. In a walkout, students stand and leave their classrooms en masse at a given time or signal. More than a million students participated in the #ENOUGH walkout.

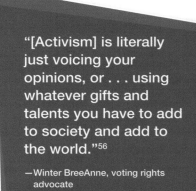

"[Activism] is literally just voicing your opinions, or . . . using whatever gifts and talents you have to add to society and add to the world."[56]

—Winter BreeAnne, voting rights advocate

BreeAnne is an example of someone who started her own project and went on to become a national leader. But BreeAnne does not see herself as an activist: "I just saw myself as playing my part in shaping the world that I want to see for our future. Young people should have a say in our future and to some that looks like activism. [Activism] is literally just voicing your opinions, or if you can't voice your opinions, using whatever gifts and talents you have to add to society and add to the world."[56]

Speak Out

The need for students to voice their opinions and use their talents for the greater good has never been more urgent. The COVID-19 pandemic proved that people throughout the world are dependent on one another, whatever their station in life. The pandemic shook society to its core and greatly increased the numbers of people who needed homes, healthcare, counseling, and other services. Millions of people volunteered to address these needs, from health care providers to students delivering meals to those living in isolation during the national emergency.

In good times and bad, society would cease to function without the active participation of its citizens, including those who are still in school. People need to be prodded sometimes to do the right thing, to educate

When teenagers put their energy into volunteering, they succeed in addressing many needs—both small and large. In the process, they also gain invaluable experience that will serve them throughout their lives.

themselves about the issues, to donate to worthy causes, and even to vote. And when teenagers draw attention to these issues, adults just might listen.

When it comes to guiding the world in a positive direction, student volunteers can heed the words of Mary Beth Tinker, a thirteen-year-old antiwar protester who was part of a landmark Supreme Court free speech decision in 1969: "If you just use the little bit of courage you have, to speak up for something you believe in, you'll be amazed at what a difference you can make. You don't have to be some great hero, some really great courageous person. . . . Just use the little bit of determination that you have."[57]

"If you just use the little bit of courage you have, to speak up for something you believe in, you'll be amazed at what a difference you can make."[57]

—Mary Beth Tinker, teen antiwar protester

Introduction: Help Needed Everywhere

1. Quoted in Tatiana Parafiniuk-Talesnick, "Why Do We Volunteer?," The Register-Guard, November 29, 2019. www.registerguard.com.

2. Megan Bailey, "How Volunteering Will Make You a Better Person," Beliefnet, 2020. www.beliefnet.com.

3. Kaleigh Rogers, "Volunteering Is the Best Kept Secret for Mental Health," Vice, December 5, 2017. www.vice.com.

4. Meghan Lynch Forder, "What Teens Gain When They Contribute to Their Social Groups," Greater Good Magazine, July 22, 2019. https://greatergood.berkeley.edu.

5. Quoted in Heather Finlay-Morreale, "Volunteering Can Help Teens Facing Emotional Challenges," *Psychology Today*, February 23, 2019. www.psychologytoday.com.

Chapter One: Volunteer Close to Home

6. Quoted in Catherine's Closet, "Making a Difference," 2020. www.catherinescloset.org.

7. Jacob Shoulders, "An Orting Resident Needs Our Help!," GoFundMe, March 23, 2018. www.gofundme.com.

8. Pet Partners, "Volunteer with Pet Partners," 2020. https://petpartners.org.

9. Quoted in Lindsey Bever, "Can This Social Challenge Actually Get Teens to Clean Up the Planet? Looks Like It's Working," *Washington Post*, March 12, 2019. www.washingtonpost.com.

10. Quoted in Bever, "Can This Social Challenge Actually Get Teens to Clean Up the Planet?"

11. Quoted in Dara Elasfar, "Youths Honored for Giving to Their Communities," *Washington Post*, May 8, 2019. www.washingtonpost.com.

12. Quoted in Melissa Driscoll Krol, "Teen of the Week: Crofton Middle School Student Started Own Organization to Help Others," *Capital Gazette*, March 8, 2019. www.capital gazette.com.

13. Operation Gratitude, "In Their Own Words: Strengthening the Fabric of Our Nation," September 30, 2019. www.operation gratitude.com.

14. Quoted in Laura Grace Weldon, "40 Ways Kids Can Volunteer, Toddler to Teen," Laura Grace Weldon, June 27, 2013. https://lauragraceweldon.com.

Chapter Two: Volunteer for a Day or Two

15. Quoted in Denton Postlewait, "25th Anniversary of Martin Luther King, Jr. Day of Service," WEAU News, January 20, 2020. www.weau.com.

16. Quoted in Postlewait, "25th Anniversary of Martin Luther King, Jr. Day of Service."

17. Quoted in Skye Hanna, "South Pas Teens Clean Parks for MLK Day," *South Pasadena (CA) Review*, January 24, 2020, https://southpasadenareview.com.

18. Quoted in Hanna, "South Pas Teens Clean Parks for MLK Day."

19. Quoted in Laura Berrios, "Douglassville Teens Take Charge of Habitat Home Build for a Veteran," *Atlanta Journal-Constitution*, January 9, 2020. www.ajc.com.

20. Quoted in Habitat for Humanity, "Volunteering Tips: Be Ready for a Habitat Build Site," 2020. www.habitat.org.

21. Quoted in Danielle Anderson, "Volunteers Scour Beaches During Flagler's Coastal Cleanup," *Daytona Beach (FL) News-Journal*, September 25, 2019. www.news-journalonline.com.

Chapter Three: Share Your Skills

22. Quoted in Megan Kamerick, "Youth Teaching Tech to Seniors Fosters Generational Connections," NPR, January 20, 2020. www.npr.org.

23. Quoted in Kamerick, "Youth Teaching Tech to Seniors Fosters Generational Connections."

24. Quoted in Kamerick, "Youth Teaching Tech to Seniors Fosters Generational Connections."

25. Quoted in Kamerick, "Youth Teaching Tech to Seniors Fosters Generational Connections."

26. Quoted in Anya Mueller, "Harmony Bridge Program Connecting Students to Seniors, with Music," Newscenter1, March 9, 2020. www.newscenter1.tv.

27. Quoted in Ruben Castaneda, "10 Interesting Ways to Volunteer at a Hospital," *U.S. News & World Report*, April 10, 2017. https://health.usnews.com.

28. Quoted in Sue Straughn, "Math Whiz Using Her Gift to Help Others," 3WEARTV, July 15, 2019. https://weartv.com.

29. Quoted in Straughn, "Math Whiz Using Her Gift to Help Others."

30. The Wheeler School, "Junior Receives National Microgrant Through United Way and Pop-Tarts," February 13, 2020. www.wheelerschool.org.

31. The Wheeler School, "Junior Receives National Microgrant Through United Way and Pop-Tarts."

32. Quoted in Keith Sharon, "O.C. Storytellers' Tales Can Reach Library of Congress via Airstream," *Orange County (CA) Register*, August 15, 2019. www.ocregister.com.

33. Quoted in Monica Humphries, "Anyone Who Needs Help Seeing Has 2 Million Pairs of Eyes Available with This App," NationSwell, April 17, 2019. https://nationswell.com.

Chapter Four: Committing to a Cause

34. Quoted in Kristina Papa, "High School Seniors Raise Awareness Locked in SPCA," WNEP, March 1, 2019. www.wnep.com.

35. Quoted in Papa, "High School Seniors Raise Awareness Locked in SPCA."

36. Matthew Bershadker, "We Are Their Voice," ASPCA, 2020. https://www.aspca.org.

37. Quoted in Patti Neighmond, "A Rise in Depression Among Teens and Young Adults Could Be Linked to Social Media Use," NPR, March 14, 2019. www.npr.org.

38. Quoted in Catherine Cheney, "It Takes a Teenager to Help a Teenager in Crisis," *New York Times*, September 24, 2019. www.nytimes.com.

39. Quoted in Cheney, "It Takes a Teenager to Help a Teenager in Crisis."

40. Quoted in YR, "Youth, for Youth," March 11, 2020. https://yr.media.

41. Quoted in Cheney, "It Takes a Teenager to Help a Teenager in Crisis."

42. Quoted in Cheney, "It Takes a Teenager to Help a Teenager in Crisis."

43. Sam Adler-Bell, "The Story Behind the Green New Deal's Meteoric Rise," *New Republic*, February 6, 2019. https://newrepublic.com.

44. Quoted in Ruairí Arrieta-Kenna, "The Sunrise Movement Actually Changed the Democratic Conversation. So What Do You Do for a Sequel?," *Politico*, June 16, 2019. www.politico.com.

45. Quoted in Sunrise Movement, "'We're Done Playing by the Rules': 20 Teens Arrested for Green New Deal Teach-in at Senate," Medium, February 17, 2020. https://medium.com.

46. Quoted in Adler-Bell, "The Story Behind the Green New Deal's Meteoric Rise."

Chapter Five: Creating Your Own Project

47. Quoted in Amy Goodman, "Meet 17-Year-Old Avi Schiffmann Who Runs Coronavirus Tracking Website Used by 40+ Million Globally," Democracy Now, March 17, 2020. www.democracynow.org.

48. Quoted in Goodman, "Meet 17-Year-Old Avi Schiffmann."

49. Quoted in Goodman, "Meet 17-Year-Old Avi Schiffmann."

50. Quoted in Jenny McCoy, "How a Simple Beach Run Sparked This Kid to Start a Nonprofit for the Homeless," Runner's World, June 18, 2019. www.runnersworld.com.

51. Quoted in McCoy, "How a Simple Beach Run Sparked This Kid to Start a Nonprofit for the Homeless."

52. Quoted in Bob Montgomery, "Adom Appiah: Founder of Ball-4Good Sets High Goals," GoUpstate.com, March 1, 2020. www.goupstate.com.

53. Quoted in Montgomery, "Adom Appiah."

54. Quoted in Gloria Barron Prize for Young Heroes, "2019 Winners," 2020. https://barronprize.org.

55. Quoted in Bridget Todd, "WHM: 17-Yr-Old Activist Winter BreeAnne Is Fighting Gun Violence," AfroPunk, March 12, 2019. https://afropunk.com.

56. Quoted in Marilyn La Jeunesse, "21 Under 21 2018: Winter BreeAnne Wants Younger Generations to Embrace the Power of Voting," Teen Vogue, November 5, 2018. www.teenvogue .com.

57. Quoted in American Civil Liberties Union of Tennessee, "Stand Up/Speak Up: A Guide for Youth Activists," 2015. www.aclu -tn.org.

Books

Chris Anderson and Lorin Oberweger, *Thank You for Coming to My TED Talk: A Teen Guide to Great Public Speaking*. New York: HMH Books for Young Readers, 2020.

Melissa Banigan, *Working with the Community in a Political Campaign (Be the Change! Political Participation in Your Community)*. New York: Rosen Young Adult, 2019.

Marke Bieschke, *Into the Streets: A Young Person's Visual History of Protest in the United States*. Minneapolis: Zest Books, 2020.

Stuart A. Kallen, *Teen Guide to Student Activism*. San Diego: ReferencePoint, 2019.

Lady Gaga, *Channel Kindness: Stories of Kindness and Community*. New York: Feiwel & Friends, 2020.

Internet Sources

Sam Adler-Bell, "The Story Behind the Green New Deal's Meteoric Rise," *New Republic*, February 6, 2019. https://newrepublic.com.

Lindsey Bever, "Can This Social Challenge Actually Get Teens to Clean Up the Planet? Looks Like It's Working," *Washington Post*, March 12, 2019. www.washingtonpost.com.

Ruben Castaneda, "10 Interesting Ways to Volunteer at a Hospital," *U.S. News & World Report*, April 10, 2017. https://health.usnews.com.

Operation Gratitude, "In Their Own Words: Strengthening the Fabric of Our Nation," September 30, 2019. www.operationgratitude.com.

Denton Postlewait, "25th Anniversary of Martin Luther King, Jr. Day of Service," WEAU News, January 20, 2020. www.weau .com.

Websites

DoSomething.org (www.dosomething.org/us). This volunteer organization is the largest nonprofit created exclusively for young people dedicated to social change. Students can find hundreds of local opportunities using the group's digital platform, which provides how-tos, inspiring stories, videos, and scholarship opportunities.

MLK Day of Service (www.nationalservice.gov). The MLK Day of Service (the third Monday of every January on Martin Luther King Jr. Day) is a time when Americans are invited to volunteer in their communities. The "Serve Your Community" link on this website displays volunteer opportunities by location that are open to all.

Operation Gratitude (www.operationgratitude.com). This organization sends care packages to military personnel, including deployed troops, new recruits, and wounded soldiers. Each package includes letters of gratitude from student volunteers and other grateful citizens. The operation's website provides instructions for interested participants.

Pet Partners (www.petpartners.org). This group runs an animal therapy program that reaches out to seniors, veterans with PTSD, patients in recovery, and others who benefit from interaction with dogs, cats, and other animals. The website contains webinars and information about volunteering in its many programs.

Volunteer Match (www.volunteermatch.org). This organization offers nearly 110,000 volunteer opportunities, categorized by location. Users can type in their city and be connected instantly with nonprofit organizations that focus on numerous worthwhile causes from children's health to literacy programs and environmental causes.

PICTURE CREDITS

Stuart A. Kallen is the author of more than 350 nonfiction books for children and young adults. He has written on topics ranging from the theory of relativity to the art of electronic dance music. In 2018 Kallen won a Green Earth Book Award from the environmental organization Nature Generation for his book *Trashing the Planet: Examining the Global Garbage Glut*. In his spare time, he is a singer, songwriter, and guitarist in San Diego.